Kissing the Long Face
of the
Greyhound

Also by Yvonne Zipter

Poetry

Like Some Bookie God (chapbook)
The Patience of Metal

Nonfiction

Ransacking the Closet
Diamonds Are a Dyke's Best Friend

Kissing the Long Face of the Greyhound

Yvonne Zipter

Terrapin Books

Terrapin Books
4 Midvale Avenue
West Caldwell, NJ 07006

www.terrapinbooks.com

ISBN: 978-1-947896-29-1
Library of Congress Control Number: 2020936426

First Edition

Cover art: *Tulip Greetings*
by Elke Vogelsang

www.elkevogelsang.com

For Kathy,
always

Contents

I

Summer Lament   7
And Then the Nap Takes Me   8
Apricot: A Love Song   10
The Nature of This   11
Hummingbird   12
The Turtles Are Sunning Themselves,   13
Cleaning Fish, Post Lake, July 1941   14
Grace Lesson   15
River Creatures   17
Into the Blue   18
Postsurgical Slumber   19

II

Naming the World   23
The Pencils Speak of Impermanence   25
One Account of How the Dead Spend Their Days   26
All Solemnity   28
Rattlesnake, Carr Fire, California, 2018   29
Envy   30
Manners of the Flesh   31
Punctuation   32
Arterial   34
Corner Store   35
Exaltation   36
Invocation   37
Night Noise   38

III

Sleep Work   43
Terribly   44
At the Siege of Leningrad Museum with Valeria   45
Anticipating This Year's Tasmanian National
     Thylacine Day   47

Elmer Almighty   49
Guarding Our Grief   50
For Want of 10 Righteous Persons   52
Kissing the Long Face of the Greyhound   53
Ein   54
Little Moon   55
Presentiment   56
Osteosarcoma: A Love Poem   57

IV

Into the Opening   61
The Death I Dream Of   62
She Never Looked So Beautiful   64
Redemption   65
Still Waters   67
Kissing Fire   68
Rosy Maple Moth   70
Running Before Dawn with the Dog   72
Preemie   73
Blue Wild Indigo   74

Acknowledgments   77
About the Author   81

Summer Lament

Catalpa blossoms clot the sidewalk
like too much joy
or an explosion of faith,
the O's of their white,
crinoline mouths
a chorus of surprise.
Already I am hating summer;
its crepey, bright days cling
like the sticky embrace
of passion's regret,
the sheets a twist
of nightmare and lust. My lover

says I complain too much.
And it's true. Here I am lamenting the carpet
of melancholy petals deadening my step,
when hours before
our dogs on the beach
(silhouettes of simplicity
in dusk dissolving to dark)
enacted bliss,
the big male's feet
tapping the water
like hammers on piano keys,
his tail a metronome of delight
(learn from this!). Hidden
in the blackness, frogs
invite me to play.

Morning, and my car is stippled
with flowers. I get in
like a bride who has forgotten the groom
and drive off, a confusion
of pale exclamations
marking my passage.

And Then the Nap Takes Me

title borrowed from James Boswell's *The Life of Johnson*

The briefest love is sometimes sweetest,
and so my ardor for the nap.
But the litany of each
that's ever cupped me in its lotus palm
would put you in a stupor,
so I will not mention

the most pitiful of naps—
that of the invalid,
who lies swathed in a blanket on the couch
while the world slips past in flickering frames—
or poorer yet, the dirt nap, the specter of which hunkers
at the end of the sofa,
tactlessly licking a mossy lip.

Better to tell of the *power nap*,
all the fashion a decade past.
Bears do it, blokes do it,
even preppy Greenwich teens do it
(let's do it—let's fall asleep).
Of course, last century we were all
hungry for power—military, electric, personal.

New to my list
is to doze upon the maple floorboards,
the narrow face of one dog
on my thigh, the head of the other
on my arm as they bathe me
in a kind of elixir
of kibble-scented breath
and the musk of waxy ears.

But easily the pleasantest of naps
is that on a Sunday afternoon—
in the summer, if at all possible—the fragrance
of new-mown lawn filtering through an open window,
a fat fly tapping at the screen,

and Pat Hughes, Voice of the Chicago Cubs,
intoning the stats like a chant,
which sets you adrift, for a moment,
like a pharaoh in a boat,
paddling toward heaven
with all the things you love.

Apricot: A Love Song

It lets me enter without reserve,
thumb meeting thumb at the crack
that arches below its stem, and then—
a parting of flesh.

It unfolds like butterfly wings
or like a book in miniature,
gives up its hard brown heart
as if it was never meant to be kept.

It measures the tongue
against its own firmness,
says sweet but hints at tart
like any seductress who knows her part.

Prunus armeniaca. Armenian plum.
Ancient Persians deemed it the egg of the sun.
The Romans thought it precocious,
an early-ripening peach.

Neither plum nor egg nor peach—
it is its own fruit, the dawn
of temptation, a blushing little butt
surrendering to my teeth.

The Nature of This

Summer squats cool and dry as a toad
on the brittle landscape,
our dreams populated
with foreign longings
for moss, mudholes, and mist.

At last, rain arrives,
tucked under the arm of a storm
as it wildly declaims to the tomato
and pumpkin plants. By morning
the garden has gone feral:
stems broken free
of stakes, tomato branches creeping
along the ground, the fruit
so nakedly voluptuous, sprawled
in the dirt, I am shamefaced.
Pumpkin vines slither
over marigolds, parsley, weeds, hungry
for experience as Edenic snakes,
and zucchini leaves paw the air for sunlight,
unconcerned for the broccoli shoots
cowering below.

This is how we enter autumn:
riding on the back of a toad,
surrendering to reckless abandon.
All around us, neighbors beat down
and tame the plant life, every blade of their lawns
emerald and shapely, the grape arbor tidy
(despite an outburst of foliage
and the unseemly dribble
of overripe berries), while we are heady
with uncontrolled life, green
to the tips of our fingers
from reaching for something unseen
in our tangle of vigor.

Hummingbird

An asterisk hangs
beside the exclamation of trumpet creeper,
the hummingbird footnotes
the billowing quiet,
the way the air or my head is clearer here—
here, where my alarm clock
is the dog poking his nose in my back;
where the lake telegraphs
peace, winking sunlight through the window
and across the scarred desk; where neighbors
and total strangers wave or nod in greeting,
and sometimes stop to chat the length of a burning cigarette
or several spacious thoughts.
The hummingbird, color of a manzanilla olive, and I,
color of red clay, hail one another
from a comfortable distance as it hovers in imitation
of a child's rendering of a star—a fury of lines
dashing from a central node. I might be holding my breath
when it shoots away and leaves me wishing on it,
leaves me spellbound, dumbstruck, reverent, leaves me
with a wild resolve to hold it
on a willowy thread of words, leaves me.

The Turtles Are Sunning Themselves,

lined up like dinner plates along a server's arm
on the log reaching up from the lagoon's shallows,
but the sliders slip from their sodden perch
into the drink the minute they sense me
on the crumbling path ringing the pond.

I wait a while, because they're worth waiting for,
hoping they'll resurface if only I'm still
as a stump. But they come by their wariness
naturally and watch me from a distance,
their necks extended like periscopes
above the water's murk.

I think what I admire
is their naked admission that our bodies
are too soft for the dangers of this world.

I stand there a while longer, ringed in shadow
by the noon sun, watching the blurred
boats of their bodies move languidly
beneath the surface like dark thoughts.

Cleaning Fish, Post Lake, July 1941

I always thought the photo of my grandfather
and his brother, with the scarred wooden table

between them on which they are gutting fish,
was about them, about the scarred woman

that came between them, but realize now
the photo is about my mother, whose arms

are no wider than the perch her uncle takes a knife to,
whose eyes are level with the metal tub on the table

where the men throw the entrails, her overalls hanging
loosely on her small frame, her shoes invisible

in the duff of leaves and pine needles, a froth of curls
around the tipped cup of her face, who isn't afraid

of the knives, the blood, the slick viscera, the bright rain
of fish scales, who isn't afraid to look at death.

Grace Lesson

In those days when it was shameful
for a woman to be so careless
as to lose a breast, my mother
wore a scar like the sign of the cross
ablaze on her chest, the edges puckered
like a narrow lip
imparting disapproval.

In those first awful months
of healing, the women's cancer
underground guided her
to an artificial breast. At an old-fashioned
ladies lingerie shop—the prosthetics
just another thing
to make a woman pretty—
I, a shy fourteen, searched
among the bustiers and brassieres
for something to look at
that didn't remind me
of loss, while the clerks,
behind a curtain with my mother—wizards
with a measuring tape—cooed
over the stitchwork
as if she were a sampler, bright
with moralization.

I imagine her afterward,
naked to the waist
in her vanity mirror,
fingering the knotted rope
up her chest, trying to arrive
at the clerks' sunny view.

When it came—the foam rubber mound, studded
with ball bearings to give the heft
of flesh—she secured it
like a keepsake

in her new bra's secret chamber,
a lifeless echo to her sound left side.

She could have let us all believe
in the redemptive power
of prosthetics. But how strange
it must have felt, that phantom heap
roaming her chest
with every movement.

In those days of shame, my mother
never let us forget, jabbing pins
into the counterfeit rise
when she sewed or imagining for us
the comedy, after swimming,
of harboring a sponge
for a bosom, how she might wring
the water from it,
as if a cleansing had occurred.

River Creatures

Perhaps, as the sleek yellow body of my kayak
glides through the river's murk, the plastic wings
of my paddles churning air and water—perhaps

the heron and turtle that eye me from the shallows
of the square-cornered North Avenue Turning Basin
think I am one of them, a denizen of Chicago's river

and its north branch canal, some large duck or
flamboyant water strider or surface-skimming
dragonfly, for they do not decamp the licked-clean

logs jutting from the silty bottom as I approach,
though they do, to be fair, keep an eye on me,
the turtle with his neck outstretched to make

a third tine on the base of the fork where he rests,
the heron bending his neck until it forms another oculus
beside the amber one in his slender blue-gray head.

I bob a few minutes more on the wind-churned water
as the three of us continue to appreciate one another
then turn my nose away to leave them to their sunning.

Into the Blue

Like angels jumping off the head of a pin,
they leap from the bridge
that fastens the river's banks
toward a boy's version of heaven, far below,
in that decade tumbling headlong toward the Depression.
As he flies, Chuck's boy-body, white
and crisp as a paper airplane,
cuts through the air,
his heart—no hint of later betrayal—
beating a symphony
of joy and terror in his ears.

The river approaches
like unavoidable temptation,
and his shock of hair
is for a moment made ruly
as he traverses the elements
into water that is cool
though not cleansing,
even in that year. The boys turn upward then,
rising to the surface
like so many Hosannas,
raucous as a band of sinners, innocents
in what passes for mischief in those days,
ready to ascend bank and girder
again. And to a bargeman downriver,
shading his eyes from the sun, they look—
in the instant after they soar again
from that sliver of metal—
like motes or sparks or, quite possibly, doves.

Postsurgical Slumber

The moon pokes out of the sky
like a troubled tooth, clouds
worrying over it like tongues
that cannot stay away,
while I follow the long red line
of my body's betrayal
through a disquieted sleep.
One expects wolves
on a night like this,
or ghosts.

You are under a different moon:
one that is full-cheeked
and auspicious
and willing to let you sleep.

But whatever paces
through *my* dreams,
restless and red-eyed,
crosses the country between us
and pulls you
to the ragged edge
of my waking,
where I am calling out
in alarm
from the dark hood
of my sleep.

Several times we make this journey,
meeting again and again, this one night,
at the border between our minds,
until at last the sun pulls the moon from the sky
and I slip away, for an hour or two,
from the path my body
and the wincing moon
have made me,

and curve beside you
like a bankless river
on the map of our sheets.

II

Naming the World

How I wish I'd been around when the world was new
and everything needed names. Now there are only puppies,
lipstick shades, and babies needing labels. Even Marianne Moore,
more than three score my senior, had nothing but cars to christen:
Mongoose Civique, Turcotingo, and Intelligent Whale—
not one of which, it seems, was what others beheld
on the drawing table. Where she saw domed roofs
and slinky low profiles, someone else recognized the Edsel.

It would be a mistake to think the early verbarian at a disadvantage,
with no desk, no pencil, no well-worn thesaurus,
with no more than an apronful of words; every man, in those days,
was turned into a poet by a world so saturated with metaphor
you had only to look at one thing
to see in it another. The secretive smirks
of mussels in their riverbed, for instance,
told another outcome for the Ark: there, at river bottom,
elephant ear, butterfly, and sheepnose,
monkeyface, fawnsfoot, elk-, and deer-, and pigtoe—the ones
that never made it to shore. A litany of mussels tallies
like pawnshop or junk-drawer inventory: pistolgrips, washboards,
pocketbooks (plain and fat), spectacle case, rabbitsfoot, and snuffbox.
So much depends on who saw what when: the wartybacks,
fat muckets, and pimplebacks burdened, through all the centuries,
with someone's bad aesthetic day. What foot
first called out *Heelsplitter*, as it found that horny shell?
And one can only suppose the face that gave refuge
to that mollusk of an orb, Higgins' eye. (Remind me
never to fraternize with Higgins!) And if the papershell,
pink or fragile or cylindrical, conjures something fine
and gorgeous, who am I to argue with that namer's vision?

And we haven't left the river yet! Think of the bird's-foot violet
lightly hopping the prairie, the walking stick out strolling the forest,
the mourning dove grieving its miserable name.
What a fever of designation there must have been

when fox and holly and dragonfly were cloaked yet
in anonymity. But for all the species nestled snug
in their taxa, a clutter still remains incognito.
Just last month, a squid, tall as a giraffe, was spied,
with fins like wings, arms like spider webs,
and so far unmonikered—the John Doe
of cephalopods. And here is my chance:
the orchid petal squid, I want to suggest,
the dulcinea, fallen angel, ivory ascot,
Flying Dutchman, or hoary mantle squid.
But the world is not so fresh now
as when we first assigned identity.
And common names—uncommonly plump, once,
with meaning—showcase now only shrinking imagination,
like whale fall stripped
to skeletons by creatures we'd surely know
as streamer or Hula-girl worms
were they discovered before the July before last.
But in a language picked clean,
all a dying whale's future holds
is being groomed
by bone-eating worms.

The Pencils Speak of Impermanence

after the photograph *Poet's Pencils,
in Memoriam*, by Gaylen Morgan

They hardly recall the trees from which they came.
Their self-hatred, how quick they are to deny their own musings.
Every day they feel diminished by their own efforts.
Their ability to hold teeth marks in their flesh
only showcases their surrender,
their willingness to be made smaller.
At their sharpest, they are notably vulnerable,
easily broken not by bruising wit
but by clumsiness and passion.
Any promise once held—potential
to create a masterpiece, to harbor genius—
has been rendered, over time, improbable
as they've shrunk in stature and come to look
like old men in their wedding suits,
huddled for company,
but who knows for how long.
Outside their cozy, they hear the familiar scrape
of something being written.
It sounds like a lame foot in a boot,
dragged across pavement.

One Account of How the Dead Spend Their Days

Say my mother's soul missed the last dirigible to heaven or,
say, despite its complex perfidy, she had grown fond
of this particular body, now stripped clean as truth,
and decided to stick around, a wisp of feeling
slipping in and out of passing grievers
like a stuttered breath. How numbing the slow drip
of days must be, the minutes sifting by like soil,
the seconds unyielding as pebbles.

Of all the senses, only hearing must survive:
why else the whispered laments of mourners?
But my mother's narrow house is quiet,
far from where we now make our homes. For her,
there is but the ghostly castanet of leaves,
the dull miserere of traffic on Lincoln. This
is how she would come to call on her neighbors,
a custom nearly abandoned by the living.
She'd have been reluctant, at first, to drop by
empty-handed. Still, the others would understand,
would be glad of the company,
tucked away as they are,
in a park where only squirrels play.

The way she'd see it, though, no need to roam far
for companionship: her second husband's
first wife is but a headstone width away.
And since their mutual husband has acted
the negligent host and not joined them,
there's nothing to impede their communication.
They would start with memories
of the house—white and stiff
as a taut sail—they both floated from this life in:
Remember the stink of oil
from the furnace, the oyster-cracker tiles in the bathroom,
the miles of moldings so enticing to the dust?
More intimate topics would follow, among them
that fist-sized hollow at the center

of their husband's chest and how each touched
or avoided it in the darkened room
at the top of the stairs.

Eventually, there would be shouting, then weeping, jealousies
and recriminations over the dissolute sons
the first wife inadvertently left behind.
(A nearby mourner would turn his head, puzzling
over an elusive sound.) Forgiveness
follows; after all,
who else do they have? They'd consider, then,
the husband, how he left them here
to cool their heels, went to Florida,
married a third time, how, as young brides,
they should have counted out the years like rations
instead of grains of rice.

All Solemnity

Birds line up on the slant of a hill,
edging forward, like a search party.
You know it must be grim:
they are all in dark suits,
with gaze turned downward.
They are combing the blades of grass
as if in an immense forest
in which someone cared for
has been lost.
You can't call out the dogs—
something about conflict of interest—
and so you just watch, as they poke
through vegetation
with the long sticks of their bills,
and offer up a prayer
of safe return or at least
an image of solace suspended
like a knotted rope up
the lonely roadside hill.

Rattlesnake, Carr Fire, California, 2018

Surely, this is how he'd like us to remember him,
raised up from his coil of muscle, meeting the threat
head on, ready to poison the flame with the needle
of his fangs. If only he could paralyze it, swallow it
whole like any other flying feathered thing. But the flame
consumed him, left a scar of char, a spiral staircase
of ribs, making of him a monument to his own valor,
his mouth now a window to the ash of our futures.

Envy

I'm rising like smoke,
a whisper of danger,

a memory of heat,
a lick of regret.

I am beautiful,
hard to contain,

ephemeral. Where
there's smoke, there's

something combustible.
I am my own secret

language, a gesture
misread, a veil dancing

against a supple sky.
The wind is my god.

I'd rather I were an atheist
like the ribbon of sock

at the bottom of the drawer,
innocent of air gusts,

content to rest.
And rest some more.

Manners of the Flesh

If I lift my eyes toward heaven,
will the rest be raised up, too?
If I press my hands in the manner of prayer,
a hitchhiker of the spirit, will I arrive?
If I kneel beside the bed of a loved one,
her body a splinter in her soul,
an ache in my heart,
a rent in the mantle of our history,
if I submit to the idiosyncratic nature
of the mind of life, which converts a gland—
the spitting image of an almond—
into a thorn, a spike, a bullet hotly seeking a mark,
if I let the salt of our collected tears
push like thumbtacks into my blank flesh,
will the reckoning of her days
do arithmetic tricks like loaf and fish
in the hands of an illusionist?
The body is a temple,
is temporary, temporal, tempestuous, untenable.
The body is an atheist, damn it,
even in war.

Punctuation

1.

As in the teleology
of syntax, there is no surprise
in finding you at the end
of every passage, giving form
to what I feel, though at the start,
you may be only an absence.

2.

In that first moment,
when scientists saw the birds dotting the field
like a thousand commas, a thousand
small interruptions in the continuity
of a long sentence about grace and splendor,
they thought the birds had been dashed
from the sky by a careless downdraft, a casting out
as of biblical sinners, turned not to pillars of salt
but to shards of silica, a sharp reminder
of our delicate marriage to a particular state
of being. From a distance—the view
my television brings me—they look like twists
of black yarn on a quilt or Van Gogh's *Starry Night,*
the birds asterisking the dark field
(the colors all wrong but the whorls precise
in their intensity): something sublime,
something you can see the hand of god in. Close in,
the story tells different, every red-winged blackbird
on its side, each beak pointed to the tainted ground, victims
in a whodunit, fingering their killers
from beyond.

3.

       It is the design
of their repose makes me think of you, yearn
to see how you landed
in that ultimate moment
of your chaotic spin

toward death. I picture your body
turned upward, open
to this one final
new experience, your arms cradling
the last of your life like a child.

Arterial

The heart is an octopus,
pulsing in the ocean
of my fluid body,
pulsing the colors
of its unseen dreams,
a stranger to light,
alone with the whoosh
of its contemplations,
safe in the shelter
of my bony breast.

Once I saw inside
a pigeon's chest,
its heart alive
with yellowjackets,
as though it were
a sticky candy,
as though it were
a sugared drink,
and the spasm
of venomous invaders
were on the lip of fall,
furiously sipping life
before, like the pigeon,
life became undone.

Corner Store

I knew it was there, but still,
what a shock, that first predawn run after its debut,
to see the open-jawed coffins at the discount casket store on Cicero,
looking especially carnivorous in the flush
of a red neon sign, never mind their toothless state.

Now, when I pass death each morning (or at least its ornaments),
I barely glance. But today, the coldest of the year so far, a fog drags itself
up the windows like breath on the frigid glass, the specter of block letters
eerily present. Here, the letter *O*, like a last gasp or astonishment
at encountering the satiny mouth. On this side,
a complete word: *hem*. A literary throat-clearing? A hint
of reluctance by some newly departed? Or recognition of the thin border
between this world and the next? And what about my mother,
amateur seamstress to the end—is she sending guidance
from the other side, disguised as sewing instruction?

Of course the alphabetical renderings are nothing more
than the ghostly remnants of the dry cleaner
that so recently left this place.
Impossible, though, not to think of the dead
when they seem so intent on writing.

Exaltation

When the universe, like a smitten lover,
surprises me with its generosity,
its play of ordinary against radiance,
the quick of me ignites like a wick,
a sizzle of light and heat
in the hurricane lamp of my body.

In the apple-snap of a November night,
I stand with the children
in the squat patch of yard while the dog,
like a silvery spirograph,
cuts teardrop loops across its corner,
her feet hammering the weary lawn,

her breath illuminating the rhythm.
The boy is on the bench,
the little girl in my arms, and the dog
turns oval after oval. We forget
to count how many times. Never
have the children witnessed such abandon

as this greyhound, this machine of muscle
and spirit, ferries in her DNA.
They laugh for all the joy of it,
for the bass beat of paws on hard earth
pounding in their chests, for the terror
of such reckless pleasure.

Invocation

Forget TV tonight, eh?
and let me find your mouth again
as if for the first time,
greedy and insatiable
as a bee for nectar,
that portent of honey.
I will let words fall away
like a reptile's used sheathing
and speak a recovered language
of nuzzle and glide and hip
and hope for transitory ignorance
of your skin, which in real life
is as known to me as my own.
I want to hear my name
on your pomegranate lips, whispered
as if in awe of its incantatory power
to wrench us out of
and dash us into
an intimacy,
to entwine us,
as if we weren't already
two stalks of flax,
bound one to the other
by wild buckwheat,
its vines blindly grasping
a shortcut to more sun.

Night Noise

The usual soughs and susurrations
of the night, interrupted
by the gnashing of teeth against wood.
The dog, a sighthound, stays curled

in the effortless circle of her sleep.
And my darling wife, a soft dune
beneath our blankets, lies as still
as a windless beach. I let them slumber,

while I rest lightly on the hammock
of their twined breathing, eyes closed,
but vigilant in the theater of sleep,
awaiting the next movement

in nature's nocturne of percussion.
The night-blackened ceiling looms,
like all the ceilings of my childhood,
floor of some improbable heaven.

No nightmares of monsters then.
They inhabited the daylight
and didn't trouble my sleep—
unlike whatever unknown creature

lurks on heaven's creaky floorboards
and gnaws at the beams of our attic.
There are people here, I want to tell it,
and I wander the dark upstairs hall

looking for a stick or pole to rap
the undersides of its feet above,
send it packing with its hunger and its need
and, possibly, some mewling kits in tow.

My sweetheart's body stirs but does not rise,
remains a rise on the relief map of our bed,
as I tap the trapdoor with a foam roller,
pretending I embody true danger.

The dog whimpers from inside her dream.
But the attic is quiet now. The streets
are quiet. And we, too, turn toward quiet,
all breath and sighs and blissful ignorance.

Sleep Work

In those earliest of days,
even sleeping was a joining together,
how we'd curl length to length
organically as whorls on a snail's shell
or press anterior to posterior
like the ribs of an angel wing clam.
Even when sleep tossed us on its restless waves,
we'd navigate the sheets, unconscious as buoys,
till we found a slack arm, a sound thigh, a musky nape—
a place to set anchor, slumber's stowaways.

Now, all too often, the business of sleep is all industry,
plumping pillows, arranging limbs,
doing peace work on the clock—
clocking out for the night shift
when we should be clocking in
for supplemental affection.

And if our bodies chance to meet,
like match head and flint,
the result is all heat, no desire,
age having made us combustible
and tired. But still, when we kiss
to seal the ribbon of another day,
even when sleep sends us drifting
to different ports, our love does honest work,
the muscle of it tethering us together.

Terribly

A blue that could burn you,
is how I remember the sky. We seemed
to be in a Mediterranean villa, white
as a salt lick. You were in the middle
of a threeway with me and a TV character,
there with us in the flesh, when, with no warning,
you turned into my mother. *This is wrong,* I thought,
still in my dream, but I let my fingertips trace
the smooth, hard tissue of her scar
up the flat plain of her chest
before wrenching myself awake. And you,
you were sick, asleep elsewhere in the house.
I would have gone to you, knelt by your side,
pressed my face into your soft, whole skin,
that resolute heat emanating from you as it always does,
if I hadn't been paralyzed
with an intimacy outstripping
even sex.

At the Siege of Leningrad Museum with Valeria

*When I heard Shostakovich's Seventh Symphony being broadcast
from the famine-stricken Leningrad I realized that we would never
be able to take it. Realizing that, I surrendered.*
> —German soldier quoted by Lyubov Tsarevskaya,
> "The Leningrad Siege"

Valeria translates from smudged pages
behind glass. *Grandma died
on 25th January, 3 pm 1942 ... Savichevs died. All died.
Only Tanya is left.* A young girl's face
looks out at us but then the cavernous room
swallows the past. We turn

a corner. Here, the man who started the museum.
From a plastic bag, Valeria pulls a photo
taken by her brother, matching
the one under glass.
A whisper of air on my neck; the past
draws closer.

The case of Lugers, tin boxes, medals
she passes without a glance and we move
to the exhibit *Leningrad Apartment, circa
1942.* She says, *I'm not supposed to do this.*
She switches off the light:
phosphorescent pins glow. Once,
Russians flickered for 900 days, heartsick fireflies,
bumping their way through blackout streets,
the canals and their fears lapping in the quiet. Winters,
all was hardened by ice.

Then, light, weak as broth from a boiled leather belt, colors
the scarred table, the metal bucket, the window's black countenance,
the heartbreaking dolly alone on the narrow bed,
the battered valise and its suggestion of passage.
There, Valeria points. *I gave them that. Mother's suitcase.*
Later, there is mother's handbag. And everywhere,
pictures of the starving. *Dead head,*

she translates from a skull-and-crossboned Nazi uniform.
Needlepoint that children made—before
or after they dug the trenches? I forget to ask—
for soldiers at the front, a sample ration of bread, smaller
than a blackboard eraser, crumbling photos,
shattered and rusted helmets crowd the displays.

Translation is no longer
necessary. Everyone understands
skin clinging to bones, a scrap of bread
you can wrap your fingers around
but costs you everything
to hold. I see Valeria see it
in my face. This isn't just history;
it's *her* history. And I am writing myself into it,
a footnote on her page.

Anticipating This Year's Tasmanian National Thylacine Day

Today the thylacine is both a wraith
and a warning, clad in a striped coat.
—Scott Weidensaul

My first encounter with a thylacine,
and it's in the pages of an article,
telling me it's extinct.
I do not take the news well,
and melancholy enfolds me,
though I bravely coped with the passing
of the passenger pigeon
and the imminent departure
of the sheepnose mussel and its kin.
But a thyla, at sixty-five pounds, is the same
as our girl dog, and I confess a longing
to pet it. How tender
it must have been, when it prized apart,
with its forty-six teeth,
the skull of a wombat,
how charming as it trotted
an echidna to exhaustion.
Who wouldn't want one?

Mary Roberts kept some in a cage,
including Benjamin,
probably the last of *her* kind,
though certainly not the first misnomered,
what with marsupial wolf,
Tasmanian tiger, and zebra dog
ventured as identifiers.
Yet *thylacine* seems wrong,
as if it might arrive with side effects,
to be listed cheerily in voiceover
and taken under doctor's orders.
Still, what's the point of quibbling
over nomenclature
when the winsome beast is gone?

But then come tantalizing reports
that thylacines may be, à la Twain,
only victims of hyperbole. Sightings happen
all the time—though, granted, one
was just a brindled greyhound,
and they've almost always been in the dark.
Occasionally, as with UFOs, a pick-up truck's
involved, though so far, there's been no mention of beer.

If I had my own, I'd let it roam free
to clean up all the vermin.
And when it came home,
it could lean upon its kangaroo tail
and open in a yawn
its amazing jaw—wide
as a bear trap—then doze
beneath the echinacea leaves,
as if its only relations
weren't the logo and coat-of-arms
that mark its celebration.

Shadows of the leaves stripe the lawn,
and I can almost see it,
forelegs curled against its tawny chest,
mouth in a sleepy grin,
though of course what I'm remembering
is the gray and wrinkled baby one
floating like a garnish in its jar of alcohol—
preserved in spirits, as the museum says,
which sets me to thinking
about souls and visions and the afterlife
and glowing eyes in the underbrush
and what's Tasmanian for *cowboy*
and whether, clinking on the seat beside him,
in some of those sightings,
there wasn't a bottle or two
of Cascade Bitter Ale.

Elmer Almighty

My grandfather was a god to me, bronzed
from secret Ashkenazi blood and tattooed
with the scars of a workingman's life.
Mechanical things perceived his supremacy
and did as he bid. Midas-like, he could transform
trash into treasure, turn Goodwill garbage
into a golden dresser graced with brass lion heads
the size of quarters biting the rings of the drawer pulls.
With his own hands, he built a house for his wife,
the pine door frames bleeding the resinous sap
of their marriage for years on end.

He rose from the hard-packed earth
of immigrant Milwaukee, an elm sapling
growing as beautiful as he was sturdy.
I see him in the attic he shared with his brothers,
breaking the glassy skin of ice
atop a chipped china bowl, mornings,
to splash glacial water on his callow cheeks.
It was so cold, he would say, with every telling,
you could see the frost on the heads of the nails,
which glinted, I imagine, like constellations
of frozen stars he could touch, so close
he was, always, to heaven.

Guarding Our Grief

It is too bright in here;
the light glares,
refuses to let us deny a thing.
Under its harsh stare, we watch
as they prepare our old tabby to die.

There is no space to comfort her
in this tiny examining room,
vet on one side, his aide on the other.
We stand stiffly off to the side
like soldiers guarding our grief.
She does not resist
as they shave her brittle leg,
barely flinches
as the needle finds the vein.
Yes, we are thinking,
we are right to be here.

The air flutters from her lungs,
her tongue slides out like a penitent's
waiting for Communion. The vet leans
to listen with stethoscope.
Her heart, he says, *is stopped. The rest
is simply reflex.*
Left to our goodbyes,
we stroke familiar mottled fur.
Still supple, she might only be sleeping.

When it is time
to take her away,
he slides his hands under,
her mu-shaped body—the curved back,
legs unbent, head and tail their logical extension—resting
in his warm, open palms.
It is now we first begin to cry.

No hand, no matter how loving or wide,
could ever carry her in life.
She always sought,
under her fragile net of ribs, the assurance
of your firmly present heart.

For Want of 10 Righteous Persons

We are all Lot's
wife now, nameless
and aimless, forced
to leave behind
what we thought
we always knew,
holding our dear
ones close, closer,
yearning for one last
look at a landscape
we'd grown to love
before it's transformed
to smoke and ash,
unrecognizable as we
are to one another.
We are immobilized,
brittle, common, sharp-
edged, corrosive,
vulnerable to fogs
and squalls and
floods and even
our own tears.

Kissing the Long Face of the Greyhound

My dog's head is the exact shape and size
of a Brooks leather bicycle saddle,
and I love to seat a kiss
on the snout of her,
bending over that jetty of face,
our heads cheekbone to cheekbone—
if a hound can be found to have cheeks—
feel the velvet of that peninsula on my lips,
the faint scent of grime and grass,
the ghost of a tongue trail
grazing her platinum fur.
The thrill of knowing we are only
the span of a sense memory
from past perfidy,
a whisker's breadth
from pointed tooth and unfurling flesh.

Ein

I am Milwaukee.
I am guttural as *Gemütlichkeit*
and open as its arms.
I am transformative as an umlaut.
I am the necklace of green that softens
a face once stern, but lifted now
toward a bluer heaven, rising
on a white wing of glass and steel.
At my core, I'm the genuine deal:
I am industry, steel-toed and gritty.
Calloused. Steady.
I am washed in the blood of printer's ink,
father to son to daughter,
a thrumming in my ears
loud as the presses on Third Street,
pressed into the service of progressives,
my people, a city's heart—
the Milwaukee River and State Street
the arteries that anchor it.
And the men before me,
my people, tapping hot lead
into the service of language.
Is it any wonder
I found my way to words?
I am looking backward, yes,
back across the years,
bitten and stained as metal slugs
in a galley tray. How else
to make my story read right?

Little Moon

All the years of my childhood,
I'd stand between my young mother
and volumes of the 1921 *Encyclopædia Britannica,*
the moldering *National Geographic*s,
behind the rocking recliner
with its wildly floral cover,
stand above the little bald spot
at the dead end of the sagittal suture—
where the Taymyr Peninsula would be
if her forehead were Canada,
her eyebrows the U.S. border.

A nickel of nearly hairless flesh
marked the cyst she'd had as a baby,
scorched away with dry ice.
All the way home in the buggy
she screamed, my grandmother loved to say,
affronted by the incivility of that din.

But in the dimly lit living room
of my grade-school years,
I only remember the quiet
as I'd stand there,
above that smooth ring of flesh,
white as a full moon
in the dark heaven of her hair,
and pluck away the stray grays
to keep her youthful.

Only now is it clear,
nearly two score years
after losing her,
that of all the silver straws
I drew, every one of them
was the short one.

Presentiment

italicized words borrowed from Sylvia Plath's
"Morning Song" and Leo Tolstoy's *Anna Karenina*

I will die in an avalanche of books,
no two alike, spines slender as iris stems,
some of them, others thick as a brick of cheese.
The pages will sigh as they settle over me
and accept me into their fold.
The dark letters on their open wings
will ink my skin. *Like a fat gold watch*
will be stamped on my breast; *happy families*
will fuse with the back of my left hand
and I will read like a mirror of what I have loved.
The deckled edges of poetry books
will remind me of speckled moths
and the late May of my life.
The unforgiving corners of hardbacks
will suggest my stepfather, the failed
military man looking for someone to command.
There will be no words for the experience.
Or maybe I mean there will be only words.
The air will be thick with dust and erudition.
The light will be weak as my eyesight.
My last breath will reek of bookbinders glue.
Live by the word, die by the word
will be my last thought. Or, no, the penultimate.
For the word *penultimate* will make me think
final pen and then, mostly, of you, my dearest,
and how you loved that word
and what was yet to come.

Osteosarcoma: A Love Poem

Cancer loves the long bone,
the femur and the fibula,
the humerus and ulna,
the greyhound's sleek physique,
a calumet, ribboned with fur
and eddies of dust churned to a smoke,
the sweet slenderness of that languorous
lick of calcium, like an ivory flute or a stalk
of Spiegelau stemware, its bowl
bruised, for an eye blink, with burgundy,
a reed, a wand, the violin's bow—
loves the generous line of your lanky limbs,
the distance between points A and D,
epic as Western Avenue, which never seems to end
but then of course it does, emptying
its miles into the Cal-Sag Channel,
that river of waste and sorrow.
I've begun a scrapbook—
here the limp that started it all, here
your scream when the shoulder bone broke,
here that walk to the water dish,
your leg trailing like a length
of black bunting. And here the words I whispered
when your ears lay like spent milkweed pods
on that beautiful silky head:
Run. Run, my boy-o,
in that madcap zigzag,
unzipping the air.

IV

Into the Opening

Going where the dogs' noses
take us—through the little woods
to the old racetrack, this particular—
this very particular—morning in June,
the asphalt oval giving way
to wildness, green pushing up
through every crevice and into this time
before the world rises. Beyond,
I let the grass run its fingers
over the naked back
of my foot. The dogs and I are drenched now
with dew and birdsong. The dogs linger
near the sling-bottomed swings,
near the valley carved in the sand
by hundreds of dangled feet.
They were on some scent, noses
sorting the breeze but, beguiled by grass,
they stop to sample the lushness.
And at such an unlikely place,
crouched beneath the framework
of play, alongside familiar paws,
two strawberries glance beneath leaves.
I pick them, red but small as peas, let them roll
onto my tongue. The grass is delicious to the dogs
in its abundance, the strawberries,
delicious in their sweet surprise, the light,
also delicious, buttery, soft, generous.
And now the loose minutes
scatter like stones at our feet
as we walk back, across the park,
through the woods,
and into the opening of the day.

The Death I Dream Of

Fiery, swift
as my car
or a 737, flashy
as a metal-capped tooth,
screeching syllables without words,
throaty

and raw, the death I dream
does not quietly cuddle
so close
that its breath,
curling
and curling
into my nose,
becomes familiar
as burnt toast.

The death I dream
is not the death my mother knew,
or her father after her,
not the death that sat
shyly for family portraits,
at our dinner table, on my mother's bed.
And I have nothing
in common with that family from downstate
born with lightning rods for spines.
What makes me think
this death will be mine?

My mouse
had a little mouse, great-grandma said
at my birth. I have lived a quiet life and fear
the noise, the flash, the spark
rushing in to fill the void. If I now raise
my voice a few decibels, dress
in yellows and reds, weave tintinnabula
into my hair, startle you

with snapping firecrackers, leave behind
these silent words for drums
and shooting skeet, it is only
to give the dazzling end
less room.

She Never Looked So Beautiful

I am thinking of how the four Danish girls
never looked so beautiful
as when they were damp with ironing,
of how Cather
appreciated this pinprick of light
into a breathtaking luminosity.
I am thinking
of the trivial moment.

The curve of the afternoon toward evening
folds the two of us in its curl,
my sister and the boys
turning toward darkness
elsewhere. From the apple tree
in the yard beyond,
pink blossoms circle
my mother's head.
She looks like a May girl
as she stands by the window, washing
potatoes at the sink.
With no more fanfare than this,
the ritual begins—
the peeler unzips
the potato skins, clacking, while I
read aloud, in my best theatrical voice,
the movie ads, especially
the racy ones. Laughter
bubbles up with the potato
water, warm and frothy. Dinners
get made this way.

I am thinking of how
she never looked so beautiful
as when her fingers were speckled
with potato juice and joy
was surging across her lips.

Redemption

My paddle dips
and cuts into the black surface,
mining gems of water, blasting them
up, into the morning air
where they hold, briefly,
the day's first timid rays of sun.
A voice carries
across the lake like a ghost
of my childhood
on another lake in another life.

In this life,
we are parting the water.
A minor miracle
how the nose of the canoe slices
like a diamond into the glassy mere,
propelled only by our own mortal muscles
and the laws of physics. All around us, seagulls stitch
their dirty white souls
to the surface of the lake
like good intentions, liable,
we know, to fly in unexpected directions.
Before us, lily pads crowd
the west end of the lake
like footprints, a blueprint
for some complex dance
of nature. We pause
among their confusion, giving physics
a rest, letting our thoughts stretch
and roam across the landscape, your voice
always behind me.

Once again, we tear into the stillness,
the broad paws and leggy stems of lilies
clutching at the oars as if they held
redemption
or at least escape

from some murky conclusion. We push through,
unsure
of our destination,
yet somehow managing
to row there together.

Still Waters

When I leave the lagoon, I know I've witnessed
something divine because in my mind, I repeat,
over and over, *Oh, my god! Oh, my god! Oh,
my god!* Below, in the reeds, an egret white
and serene as a feathered angel.
Resting on the half-submerged branch
of a fallen tree, a cormorant.
And a turtle, a corrugated halo of tranquility,
mere feet from the bank where my feet are planted,
meets my gaze before slipping from view
like a vision slowly fading. *Did I really
just see that?* You can keep your rising
from the dead, your five thousand loaves
and fishes. There is wonder enough for me
in the slender dagger of an egret's beak,
its gold-ringed eye, judging me.

Kissing Fire

1.

Our lips are so dry, she says, *we could start a fire,*
kissing. Once, we were incendiary as match tips,
any flick of skin on skin, a conflagration,
a curtain of flame through which we saw the world.
Something as coy as oxygen fed us,
our bodies the proverbial two sticks rubbed in concert.
And wasn't it exciting? But fire never holds still,
never latches onto a sole identity.
Like when the dollar-store factory caught fire
and the flames changed complexion
with every new pallet of trinkets
they pressed their tongues to,
chameleons gauging mood by mouth.

2.

Scoff, if you will, at the stupidity of moths,
flying doggedly into the heat of their own deaths,
but when that fire flowered beside the railroad tracks
like an awful poppy, we spilled from the doors
of homes and cars and the 78 bus,
as phototaxic as any bug that ever kissed the blue light.

3.

Suppose the campfire's flicker gestured
like the hands of an Arabian dancer,
liquid and hypnotic, training the eye
to its breathtaking center.
Suppose the conflagration,
caressed by its necklace of stones,
dissolves the sound of those other children,
the grandfather, the whip-poor-will
at the lip of Toothaker's farm,
the wind in the pines
and the pines themselves.
Why, then, should it surprise us

when the boy, seated atop the picnic table,
tumbles forward, head over heels in a daze,
into the fire's warm embrace?

4.

I am the first to put out the light,
press my face to the pillow,
nesting there like a dog in its pile of rags.
I feel a familiar body, then, lean across
from the opposite side of the bed,
familiar words fall upon my ear,
familiar lips touch lightly to my cheek.

I tell you this, young lovers:
the fire is a liar, a ravishing fiction
that diverts notice from the unassuming ember,
which knows a thing or two about how to linger.

Rosy Maple Moth

I see the way you look at me,
like I am false, a pretender,
like I am, somehow,
a liar. Just because
I did not choose
the sack cloth–and–ashes look
of my homespun cousins (hysterics
or would-be saints,
always throwing themselves
into a cleansing fire) does not mean
I have never been unhappy
with my lot. If I admire
the glamour of the lacy wings
of mottled peonies
or the fat yellow sex
of certain other flowers,
if I dust my tapered body golden,
soft as a cone of pollen, and drape myself
in pink and white scarves of silk,
do not think for a moment
that in my heart I yearn to be
not-moth.

Who are you to judge, you
who have never marched
in formation by yourself,
the love child
of Frankenstein
and a millipede? If I now vamp and preen,
it is because I can finally
inspire gasps of awe, not horror. I have come out
of my shell. I am done
with hiding myself
away. I have discovered
my own beauty and will guard it
to the end, so that even
when you find me clinging
to a window screen against

the pull of death, wings ruffled only
by a breeze,
you will surprise yourself
by taking note
of a moth.

Running Before Dawn with the Dog

His legs are made for this, tensile
as bungee cords and nothing wasted, while mine
are an embarrassment of excess, a tangle
of misspent evolution. We set out
from the porch stairs, the shush
of cars on Cicero Avenue
compelling the nearby houses into silence. He glides
beside me, each filament
of his ropy body tuned,
from his years on the racetrack,
to the presence of small game. Only a month
he's been with me, and already we move like gears
in a music box. He wears the night
over his muscled frame and would fade
from me wholly if not for the Milky Way
of white fur dotting
his long snout. His tags
are the melody we run to, nearly
the only sound; the bark
of a house-bound dog
stands in counterpoint. My murmurs must fall
like gentle waves over his ears, a steady rhythm
of praise and instruction. We slip
like a stream through the reservoir
of predawn light,
barely a ripple.

Preemie

When I was your age,
I wasn't even born yet.
No one knew what to call me,
how many limbs I'd have,
if my heart would be sound,
whether I'd have hair
or await delivery of it later.
I didn't know half what you know—
how to breathe, cry, suckle,
how to use the touch of my mother's skin
as a pacifier or a call to belong.
I hadn't yet faced the cracking open
of a fresh day, its slow golden seeping
into the homecoming of night's womblike embrace.
Though you were smaller than a sack of flour,
dwarfed by your mother's hand in the NICU,
you knew things she didn't know:
that the wordless prayers of survival
she breathed in rhythm
with the rise and dip of your back
were a kind of music
and that, behind the veil
of your terrycloth eye shields,
your eyes burned as blue
as any pilot light.

Blue Wild Indigo

italicized line borrowed from Catherine E. McKinley's
Indigo: In Search of the Color That Seduced the World

I have long admired their dark oval bodies,
wagging like chow tongues in the breeze.
Yet for all the pods' deep bruise of color,
it's the plant's modest, green elliptical leaves,
with their secret concentrations of indican
(tryptophan's less sleepy cousin),
that yield the dye prized, once, by shamans,
slavers, rag traders, and kings, the powder
that *was more powerful than the gun,*
that was worth, in a length of cloth,
a human body. It's the pod's interior, though,
that's the real marvel to me, seeds lined up
like piglets at suckle, like rowers in a scull,
like socks in a gentleman's drawer, like
footlights glowing golden against the pod's
black backdrop, ready to illuminate the next
stage of their cycle: heroes of their own story.
The two halves of a pod rest side by side on my desk
like pages of an open book about some captives,
making their escape in two rough-hewn boats.

Acknowledgments

I gratefully acknowledge the following publications in which a number of these poems first appeared, some with different titles:

Bellingham Review: "All Solemnity" (as "All Solemnity on a Sunny Day"), "And Then the Nap Takes Me"

Calyx: "Hummingbird" (as "Summering"), "Naming the World"

Common Ground Review: "Kissing the Long Face of the Greyhound," "Still Waters"

Comstock Review: "Terribly"

Educe: "Invocation"

Escape into Life: "Cleaning Fish, Post Lake, July 1941," "Little Moon," "Night Noise"

Evergreen Chronicles: "Guarding Our Grief"

Fogged Clarity: "Kissing Fire"

Heron Tree: "Blue Wild Indigo," "For Want of 10 Righteous Persons"

Independent Variable: "The Turtles Are Sunning Themselves"

Isotope: "Anticipating This Year's Tasmanian National Thylacine Day"

Mediphors: "Postsurgical Slumber"

Metronome of Aptekarsky Ostrov: "At the Siege of Leningrad Museum with Valeria"

modern words: "Redemption"

Mud Season Review: "Sleep Work"

Pittsburgh Poetry Journal: "Elmer Almighty"

Poetry: "Osteosarcoma: A Love Poem"

Primavera: "The Nature of This," "One Account of How the Dead Spend Their Days"

Rufous City Review: "Ein"

San Pedro River Review: "Exaltation"

Sinister Wisdom: "Apricot: A Love Song" (as "Apricot: A Love Poem")

Southern Humanities Review: "Preemie," "Manners of the Flesh"

Spoon River Poetry Review: "The Death I Dream Of," "Grace Lesson," "Into the Blue," "Punctuation," "Rosy Maple Moth," "Running Before Dawn with the Dog," "She Never Looked So Beautiful," "Summer Lament" (as "Summer Poem")

"Grace Lesson," "Manners of the Flesh," and "Osteosarcoma: A Love Poem" were reprinted in *Sequestrum: Literature and Art.*

"Kissing the Long Face of the Greyhound" was reprinted in *A Constellation of Kisses,* ed. Diane Lockward (Terrapin Books, 2019).

"Osteosarcoma: A Love Poem" was reprinted in *Writing and Understanding Poetry for Teachers and Students: A Heart's Craft,* eds. Suzanne Keyworth and Cassandra Robison (Rowman & Littlefield, 2015).

"The Pencils Speak of Impermanence" was published in *Fading Light: Open to Interpretation,* ed. Anastasia Faunce (Taylor & O'Neill, 2013).

"Anticipating This Year's Tasmanian National Thylacine Day," "Into the Opening," "Running Before Dawn with the Dog," "Summer Lament" (as "Summer Poem"), and "And Then the Nap Takes Me" appeared in the chapbook *Like Some Bookie God* (Pudding House Publications, 2006).

"Grace Lesson" received an Illinois Arts Council Literary Award in 2001.

I also want to express my gratitude for feedback I've received on individual poems from many longtime friends, including Mike Brehm, Linda Bubon, Amy Carbone, Mary Nell Hoover, Jane Jiambalvo, and Maureen Sweeney. Finally, I am deeply grateful to Kathy Forde, Mary Leas, and Maureen Talbot for helping me think through the arrangement of poems in this book.

About the Author

Yvonne Zipter is the author of the full-length collection *The Patience of Metal* (Hutchinson House), which was a Lambda Literary Award Finalist, and the chapbook *Like Some Bookie God.* Her poems have appeared in numerous periodicals, including *Poetry, Southern Humanities Review, Bellingham Review,* and *Spoon River Poetry Review*, as well as in several anthologies. She is also the author of two nonfiction books, *Diamonds Are a Dyke's Best Friend* and *Ransacking the Closet*. A retired manuscript editor for the University of Chicago Press, she lives in Chicago, where she has shared her home with a number of retired racing greyhounds over the years.

CPSIA information can be obtained
at www.ICGtesting.com
Printed in the USA
LVHW090528030820
662234LV00001B/69